Induction:
poems for my new daughter

poems by

Colleen Alles

Finishing Line Press
Georgetown, Kentucky

Induction:
poems for my new daughter

ACKNOWLEDGMENTS

"Lullaby" was selected as the Poetry Society of Michigan's 3rd place finisher
in the society's annual poetry contest (category: anaphoric poems), August
2016. It appears in the Fall 2016 issue of *Peninsula Poets: Contest Edition*
(73-2).

All other poems previously unpublished.

Publisher: Leah Maines
Editor: Christen Kincaid
Cover Art: Dustin Tinney
Author Photo: Megan Davis
Cover Design: Elizabeth Maines McCleavy

Printed in the USA on acid-free paper.
Order online: www.finishinglinepress.com
              also available on amazon.com

Author inquiries and mail orders:
Finishing Line Press
P. O. Box 1626
Georgetown, Kentucky 40324
U. S. A.

Table of Contents

for Mara

Geography

When someone tells me
you look like me,
I think about

how the ancient glaciers
of every ice age cut channels
                        through mountains,
                        across continents,
finally settled down
as seas.

I think about how sometimes
those waters pushed land masses
away from one another—
often very far apart.

And how if you look closely
at the coastlines,
you can see
that all bodies of land

once belonged
only to
each other.

Two Balloons

"Releasing a balloon: hope."
~Tony Crisp, "Dream Dictionary"

They told me you were a girl
because I carried you high,
craved chocolate croissants.

I knew you were a girl
because twice I had this dream:

Your father stood before me,
      a pink balloon in one hand,
      a blue one in the other.

He smiled at me
like he knew something

as the string of the pink balloon
slipped through his fingertips.

I watched the pink balloon
float past my face,
ascend with all my joy,
carry me away.

Houseguest

When I was waiting to learn if
you'd be here by summer,

the number 5—my lucky number—
began to appear everywhere.
And then twice in the same day, the clock face
showed me the exact minute my father was born: 10:38.

In fact, it was like a dozen
superstitions, omens, and signs
of good fortune had knocked at my door
and I had let them all in.

At night, I would round
my belly with my fingertips,
numbering the signs each day:

I saw my mother's favorite bird three times
in the same week. A ladybug landed
on my hand as I reached for the morning paper.

The name of that waitress, the bright peonies—
both of which had belonged to my grandmother.

I even plucked a dull penny off the sidewalk
coming home from a long walk.

I drew a hot bath, stripped down naked,
let my tired limbs sink under the water for a soak.

Then almost as an afterthought, I threw
the coin into my homemade wishing well,

whispered to all the Superstitions
and Signs and Omens and Fates
and Gods of Good Fortune
who would listen:

Please tell my daughter she is invited
into this old body, too.

Early Spring

All of us were thrilled with Spring's early arrival.
Winter was pulling back her arctic fingers. They
had gripped our bodies since December.

That is, until the melting snowbanks
and the pooling ice and the damn hound dog
tripped me on my evening walk. I slipped, and

I landed on my back, and all I could think was
that Oscar Wilde told us we are *all* flat on our backs
in the gutter, but some of us are looking at the stars.

I cursed Oscar, then Charlie. I made Charlie
run home with me, dragging and choking him,
the soggy mud so thick it threatened to swallow our feet.

Flat on my bed, I cursed some more,
holding my breath and my belly in my hands
and I cried—

and everything was gutter
until I could feel you move again,
until the panic and the fear retreated like Winter,

and I let that damn dog spread mud all over
the ivory comforter, lick away the tears
until I could see those Wilde stars again.

An Aside

On the refrigerator, there is a picture
of you wrapped in a polka dot
blanket. Your eyes are closed.
You are just brand new.

Your hands are clasped, folded
together under one cheek, like you are lost
in the middle of a sideways prayer.

But really, the prayer is mine:

Please take care of this
perfectly wrapped gift.
Please look after this girl.
Keep her safe.

Share her with me for just the longest
of time.

Induction

I made a lovely cup of tea today.

The coral kettle whistled at me
from the kitchen
(and no one has whistled at me
in a while).

I poured the water into a fresh mug
and nearly fainted from exhaustion, or the scent
of lemongrass and ginger root—
a shadow of orange, just a touch
of hibiscus.

I might have been sheltered by a thousand
steady trees in a secluded meadow, or deep
in a farmer's field, lost among
the neat rows of his ready harvest.

Or on any coast at all. Let's say
Ireland, with her devastating cliffs and rich-
to-the-bone green—

Like when I walked the stony streets
of Dublin, and that blue-eyed Irishman
held the door for me, appraised me with his gaze
like I was the holiday he'd been waiting all year
to take himself on.

But I don't know.
I never drank that lovely tea.

I found it hours later, ice cold
in the kitchen. I had left it,
and the meadow, and the field, and the coast,
and the Irishman

to hold instead my newborn daughter,
my hands cupped around
the warmth of her head,

a hint of citrus
floating from her hair.

Lullaby

Since Tuesday, tiny bulldozers
have been tearing away at that house down the street.
You know the one. Chipped paint, sagging eaves.
The one with no front door.

I see the house in spurts and shifts because
our giggling daughter is pulling the curtains open and shut
as I rock her in her chair. It's 3 p.m., and although she disagrees,
she needs to nap. She wants to play,

since she's big enough now to make things move.
And because sleep is such a distant shore, I start laughing
too, listening to her, listening to the white noise machine
we bought to help her sleep. It plays the sound of the ocean.

I see that light lock of hair behind her ear. I kiss her hairline
and take in a deep wave of her as we rock back and forth,
back and forth. And suddenly I am thinking about my
grandmother, wondering if *her* house will be torn down,

since it's caving and old, too. My grandparents moved to the farm
after World War II, when people made commitments like that. To
land. To one another. I keep rocking our daughter, and peeking at
that house, and

I see in my memory my grandmother swaying in church,
back and forth, back and forth—and I see our girl is finally
giving way to sleep, her breathing steady, but
drowned out by the sound of that white noise ocean. And

since I'm sure they'll build something else down the street,
in place of that house, and since someday, I'm sure
my grandmother's house won't stand on that land anymore,
I will let our daughter nap in arms for now.

Mara

Because I named you for the sea,
I wasn't surprised to see:
you loved the feel of dark lulling waves
on your skin, the lapping water flowing
sometimes unpredictably to your chin.
That first time we swam together.

But despite your excitement, you still
wrapped your legs around my body,
clung snugly to me, the way I wonder
you did when you swam inside of me,
when I was your whole ocean.
When I was your entire sea.

Recipe Box

At one time
it had seemed important to me
to copy my mother's recipe collection
onto 4x6 pastel index cards:
        green for salads,
        pink for desserts.

It took me hours to mimic her precise cursive script,
ink her ingredients, measurements, instructions.

I filed the cards in a small cedar box
adorned with carved flowers, birds, more cursive script.
I wanted to create my own tribute to her dinners, my own
museum of a hundred perfect meals.

And then lost
in a daydream or a memory or a thought,
I looked down to see my daughter
        only a few hundred days old herself

sitting on the kitchen floor, surrounded
by piles of colorful cards,

bending and folding and tearing the recipes,
grinning and laughing
at me and my perfect recipe box,

reorganizing all that work, and
reordering
in the process
my beautiful life.

Wild Ride

I.

Five wild boys wearing jerseys, shorts in November
cycle by me as I wait curbside for the bus.

I watch them wobble, whiz, whir
from sidewalk to street, sidewalk to street.

Looking back, one laughs at me.

When the southbound number six
roars down the road a moment later, it nearly hits him.

The driver catches my eye as if to say,
Why are you letting them ride like that?
This is so dangerous.

I sigh at the driver, shrug under my coat.
These are not my wild boys, I think.
They are not mine.

II.

Tonight is the first night I am away
from my daughter
in the six months she has been my daughter.

I look up at the sky and the trees that
are losing their leaves to the changing season
and I think,

Why have I let that girl out of my sight?
Why would I *ever* let her out of my sight?
This is so dangerous.

I shrug my shoulders again.

She is my daughter, but
she will have a wild ride all her own.
She is my girl, but she is also not mine.

Laundry

You haven't done this to me in months:
woken me in the exact middle of the night.

I heard you crying, crept to your room.
I rocked you as though we were slow dancing
to an unheard, invisible song.

Your hands tighten on my shoulder and I find
I don't exactly mind the interruption from sleep,
the excuse to sway with you.

And I don't even mind the middle-of-the-night thoughts
that now slip into my mind, like a pile
of dirty laundry demanding to be reckoned with.

I squeeze you close, because
what if you were pulled from a dream
by a middle-of-the-night thought
like this one:

Someday, when all our nights and days are done,
how will our two souls know one another?
Will they have to work hard to find each other?

And when they reunite, will it feel just as wonderful
as this exact moment—

your gentle breath on my cheek, your tiny sigh.

Will it feel like summer,
        like sunshine,
        like clean sheets?

What about this, Baby:

Maybe we will feel like two matching socks,
separated once,
cycled apart for a time,

but eventually paired together again,
folded into each another, and
gently laid down as one.

Bubbles

Yeah.
I know.

                              I wish they would last
                                    a few more seconds
                                    before popping
                                    on your arm.

            Hell—I wish
            it all lasted
            longer
            too.

Pillow

Before you were out here, you
lived in the space under my lungs, my ribs—
where my bones protected you.
Where I couldn't leave you like house
keys as I rushed out the door.

I always remembered you
the way I remember
to bring my own heart
wherever it is I am supposed to go.
And also to some places I just want
to be.

You are fighting a fever tonight.
I'm rocking you in your chair.
Your torso presses against
my stomach, my chest.

Your deep sigh tells me maybe you miss
those days, too, that maybe you wish
I would stretch my skin over you like a tarp,
take you back inside

to sleep
in the shelter of my body.

Let's ask these old bones if they'd
tent around you,
allow you to rest in here,
your body in my body,
the heavy weight of your cheek
resting on my heart.

Sixteen Months

I'll admit I don't always know
what to do with you.

Though it's different now from
         the early days when
         all there was for you
was sleep and hunger
and shapes and sounds
and colors.

And me: my body
         my scent
         my warmth.

One piece of advice I recall
sharply from the baby book says
never let a loud noise or really
anything at all scare you—the baby.

(Seems like good advice for anyone
though.)

Now, your feet almost reach
the tricycle pedals, and there are
new ways I'm stymied.

How to get you to stop pulling my hair
and thinking it's funny.
(Although it is a little funny.)

How to get you to stop planting
your feet in the dog's water, or dip
your paci in the toilet bowl—

and how to be less cavalier
about staircases.

Now, I don't always know
what to do with you on very long afternoons
when everything feels exhausted,
and my best idea

is to hum Johnny Cash,
take you out to the front yard
where we pick and pull at patches
of the overgrown lawn,
catch the occasional weed
in our fingers.

I have to wonder
          if teaching you
          to uproot so much grass
          is good advice or bad,

and while I'm trying to decide,
I finally remember all the words
to *Rose of My Heart*,

and I sing them to you as we throw
ripe blades into the air,

let them fall like confetti
onto our shoulders,
into our hair.

Sweet Potatoes

I write
all over,
in my journal,
however I am feeling.

Wasteful.

Big letters.
Skipped lines, generous margins.

But at the store where I bought the notebook,
there were
a hundred just like it. A bevy of pens, too.

What if
paper became rare
(like it used to be, for people, long ago),
and ink exotic
(like it used to be, for people, long ago).

I wonder how I'd
write if I only had one page.

Would I spend three paragraphs on such a stupid thing
as a frustration at work, a trivial
argument with my husband, the need
the house has for an
air duct cleaning?

Or would I stop.

Write slowly
with careful letters:

Tonight
I fed my daughter
warm hunks of sweet potatoes off my fingers,
and she leaned into my hands like a hungry bird,
smiling between bites,
beating my heart in
the process.

Colleen Alles is a native Michigander living in Grand Rapids. She completed a BA in English with an Option in Creative Writing from Michigan State University, and also earned her master's from Wayne State University. Her fiction and poetry have appeared in literary magazines and other publications, including *Red Cedar Review, Peninsula Poets, Cardinal Sins, Write Michigan 2016 Anthology*, and others. She works for a public library in West Michigan. When not writing, Colleen enjoys spending time with family, running, traveling, baking, good coffee, and craft beer.

www.ingramcontent.com/pod-product-compliance
Lightning Source LLC
LaVergne TN
LVHW021127080426
835510LV00021B/3348